AF415556

Caution !
ONLY READ THIS BOOK
IF YOU ARE 100%
DEDICATED TO
SURRENDERING TO
GOD.

Faith Over Habit: A Biblical Path to Freedom from Smoking

Listance M Mutukudzi

Published by Listance M Mutukudzi, 2024.

FAITH OVER HABIT: A BIBLICAL PATH TO FREEDOM FROM SMOKING

First edition. November 28, 2024.

ISBN: 979-8230538066

Written by Listance M Mutukudzi.

Table of Contents

Faith Over Habit: A Biblical Path to Freedom from Smoking...........1

Chapter 1..4

Chapter 2..7

Chapter 3..9

Chapter 4.. 19

Chapter 5.. 24

Chapter 6.. 26

Chapter 7.. 29

Chapter 8.. 32

Chapter 9.. 38

Chapter 10 40

Chapter 11 43

Chapter 12 47

Chapter 13 50

I dedicate this book to YOU.

Psalms 34: 6-8

6.This poor man cried, and the LORD heard him, and saved him out of all his troubles.

7. The angel of the LORD encampeth round about them that fear him, and delivereth them.

8. O taste and see that the LORD is good; blessed is the man that trusteth in him.

Topics

Description of Faith Over Habit: A Biblical Path to Freedom from Smoking

1. The Power of God's Divine Way: When God takes over
2. Introduction: Embracing the Journey to Freedom
3. Preparation and Commitment: 5 Key Strategies for Breakthrough
4. Understanding Smoking Addiction: The Physical and Psychological Effects
5. The Power of Faith: Tapping into Divine Strength
6. Renewing the Mind: Cultivating a Smoke-Free Mentality
7. Free from Bondage: Breaking the chains of illusions
8. Coping with Triggers and Temptations: Strategies for Emotional Resilience
9. Overcoming Obstacles: Navigating Social Pressures and Peer Influence
10. Building Healthy Habits: Positive Lifestyle
11. Staying Committed: Maintaining Long-Term Success in Smoke-Free Living
12. Looking Forward: A Life Transformed by Faith Over Habit
13. Prayer Points

Description of Faith Over Habit: A Biblical Path to Freedom from Smoking.

Hebrews 11:1 "Now faith is assurance of things hoped for, a conviction of things not seen."

In "Faith Over Habit: A Biblical Path to Freedom from Smoking," readers will embark on a transformative journey towards breaking free from the chains of smoking addiction. This empowering self-help guide delves deep into the physical, psychological, and social aspects of quitting smoking, offering a comprehensive approach backed by biblical wisdom, actionable strategies, and unwavering support.

Drawing on the power of faith, this book goes beyond traditional self-help methods by integrating spiritual principles into the journey of overcoming smoking addiction. Through relatable personal anecdotes, expert insights, and scriptural guidance, readers will discover a renewed sense of hope, strength, and purpose in their quest for freedom from tobacco.

"Faith Over Habit" recognizes that quitting smoking is not merely a matter of willpower or habit-breaking techniques; it requires a holistic approach addressing the physical cravings, emotional triggers, spiritual warfare and societal influences that often hinder progress. With this understanding in mind, readers will navigate a carefully crafted roadmap designed to empower them with the tools needed to overcome challenges and build a solid foundation for lasting change.

Each chapter explores different facets of the smoking cessation process, providing practical advice and strategies for managing withdrawal symptoms, coping with stress and cravings, and developing healthy habits. Intertwined throughout are relevant biblical passages that illuminate the importance of faith, resilience, and determination as valuable allies on the journey towards freedom.

Whether you have recently made the decision to quit smoking or have struggled with addiction for years, "Faith Over Habit: A Biblical

Path to Freedom from Smoking" hopes to offer a refreshing perspective that combines science-backed strategies with the timeless wisdom of scripture. Prepare to be empowered, inspired, and equipped as you embark on this life-changing journey towards a smoke-free life driven by faith and determination.

Romans 12:2 "Do not conform to the pattern of this world, but be transformed by the renewing of your mind. Then you will be able to test and approve what God's will is—his good, pleasing and perfect will." GOD BLESS YOU.

Chapter 1
The Power of God's Divine Way: When God takes over.

Psalms 28:7 "The LORD is my strength and my shield; my heart trusts in him, and he helps me. My heart leaps for joy, and with my song I praise him."

Incorporating spirituality into your life brings God closer and invites divine intervention. It allows you to surrender your challenges and rely on Him. He hears your hopes, fears, and struggles, and in exchange, our loving Lord provides:

1. Divine strength that exceeds our own abilities. Psalm 118:14
2. Provide comfort, Deuteronomy 31:8-9
3. Hope, Romans 12:12
4. Protection, 2 Thessalonians 3:3
5. And the ultimate unwavering support. Psalm 54:4

God will be all of the above for you, the sufferer, through the difficulties of quitting smoking. At the end, not only will you be free from addiction but you will be closer to Him and gain a deeper understanding of how faith can and should be a driving force in your life. God knows when it's time, so let Him lead you and surely you will conquer.

In "Faith Over Habit," you'll find practical strategies to improve your faith in God. Prayer, fasting, worship, and scripture reading are the primary practices/activities for strengthening one's relationship with God. By truly engaging in these practices regularly and earnestly, one can cultivate a sense of inner peace and fortitude that aids in their journey towards freedom from smoking and thereafter. You can also apply the same principles to other aspects of your life.

Church Services

Matthew 18:20 "For where two or three gather in my name, there am I with them."

Attending church services can also provide important spiritual support as you strive to quit smoking. Church gives an opportunity for communal interaction, collective prayer, and maybe shared experiences with others on the same journey. It provides a sense of belonging and reminds us that we are not alone in our struggles.

Participating in prayer, fasting, worship, or bible study will help to enhance your spirituality and create a supportive atmosphere for growth. Seek out communities where you feel welcome and understood, where fellow believers may inspire and encourage you on your own path to smoke-free living.

Colossians 3:16 "Let the message of Christ dwell among you richly as you teach and admonish one another with all wisdom through psalms, hymns, and songs from the Spirit, singing to God with gratitude in your hearts."

A prayerful life allows you to connect with God. It allows you to convey your deepest desires, fears, and struggles to God. Through prayer, you can receive comfort in knowing that you are not alone in your battle. God provides you strength. Prayer, combined with worship and Bible study, connects your heart and mind with divine guidance, providing strength, and encouragement along the road. Trust that God hears your prayers and will provide you with the help and direction you need to overcome your smoking addiction.

Action Point: Make a list of specific daily prayer points and bible verses tailored to overcoming smoking addiction. See Chapter 13, to get you started.

Prayer Point: Include your prayer points and Bible verses in your prayer sessions. You are advised to recite these Bible passages and prayers during periods of weakness or temptation, reminding yourself of why you want to quit and praying for divine intervention to help you overcome any obstacles.

Chapter 2

Introduction: Embracing the Journey to Freedom

Luke 21:19 "Stand firm, and you will win life."

Having a positive mindset and determination are essential factors in successfully quitting smoking. The road to freedom from smoking addiction is not an easy one, but with the right attitude and unwavering determination, it is achievable. We can learn from Luke 21:1-19, Jesus is telling his disciples of the evils to come during, **"The Destruction of the Temple and Signs of the End Times"**. I believe hearing about the wars, earthquakes and persecution of believers must have induced indescribable fear into the disciples, just as much as the idea of quitting smoking does to a smoker, as irrational as it sounds.

But Jesus goes on to comfort and encourage his disciples as I do you now, by saying, **"14 But make up your mind not to worry beforehand how you will defend yourselves. 15 For I will give you words and wisdom that none of your adversaries will be able to resist or contradict. 19 Stand firm, and you will win life."**

It is crucial to believe in your ability to overcome this addiction. Determination and resilience play a significant role in your journey to quit smoking. There may be moments of doubt or temptation, but with faith, you can stay committed to your goal. It's important to remind yourself of why you decided to quit and the positive changes it will bring to your life.

Throughout this book, you will find the guidance and support needed to embrace the journey towards freedom from smoking addiction. Remember that you are not alone on this journey. Many have successfully quit smoking, and with faith, determination, and the support of others, you can too.

As we move forward, let us explore practical strategies, biblical wisdom, and expert insights that will empower you on this transformative path. Prepare yourself mentally and emotionally for the challenges ahead, knowing that with a positive mindset and determination, victory over smoking addiction is within reach.

Bible Reading and Prayers

Take a moment to read these bible verses, meditate on them and pray.

Understand Your Identity in Christ

2 Corinthians 5:17: "Therefore, if anyone is in Christ, he is a new creation. The old has passed away; behold, the new has come."

Quitting smoking starts by understanding that your identity in Christ gives you the strength to overcome any addiction. God sees you as His beloved, capable of breaking free from harmful habits.

1 Corinthians 6:19-20: "19 Do you not know that your bodies are temples of the Holy Spirit, who is in you, whom you have received from God? You are not your own; 20 you were bought at a price. Therefore, honor God with your bodies."

Prayer point: Spend some time reflecting and praying about who you are in Christ—a new creation. Recognize that your identity isn't defined by smoking or any addiction but by God's love and purpose for you. Thank Him for giving

Chapter 3

Preparation and Commitment: 5 Key Strategies for Breakthrough

This book is my testimony and a reminder to myself on how my faith in God helped me overcome a smoking addiction.

When we hear stories of people who overcame addiction via faith, we want to know how they did it and follow in their footsteps. These stories reveal God's transformative power and how using it can help you break free from the bonds of addiction. So, I am hoping that my process can benefit someone else.

I encourage you to start by believing that triumph over smoking is possible through faith. It is a key step in the smoking cessation process. In this chapter, we will discuss the elements that are essential to triggering a complete and permanent transformation.

Romans 8:37 - "No, in all these things we are more than conquerors through Him who loved us."

1. Fasting

1 Corinthians 9:27- "But I discipline my body and keep it under control, lest after preaching to others I myself should be disqualified."

Biblical fasting is vital for members of the body of Christ; it is necessary, among other things, to deal with the flesh. Apostle Paul said: But I keep it under my body and bring it under control.

What is fasting and when to fast?

Fasting refers to abstinence, and Biblical fasting entails refraining from food and drink or both for an extended length of time.

Fasting is the act of depriving oneself of things that give one pleasure in order to subdue the flesh and strengthen the spirit. In Matthew chapters 3 and 4, Jesus is baptized; He goes into the wilderness to fast for 40 days; after being tried by the devil and coming out triumphant, He begins His ministry. Jesus' 40-day fast emphasizes the need and benefits of fasting as we prepare for major life challenges.

There are numerous scenarios why people fast, but this book will only address two since they are pertinent to addiction treatment. The first scenario: when preparing for a large undertaking or endeavor etc. Matthew.4:1-3. This fast will help you prepare psychologically, spiritually, and physically to overcome your addiction. The second purpose: when seeking God's intervention e.g 2 Chronicles 20: 3-10. He will give you strength and change your life as you begin your journey to quit smoking.

Fasting was one of the strategies I utilized to combat and overcome my addiction. If you are truly determined and ready to break free from addiction, I believe you should begin by fasting, just as Jesus fasted and received the power to overcome temptation.

Fasts can be divided into two:

1. Absolute Fasting: Is abstaining from food and water for a specified period of time. After three days, it is medically recommended to drink water.

1. Normal Fasting: A fasting individual can eat after 24 hours. Water may be consumed in intervals, depending on the length of the fast.

The benefits and results of fasting: Isaiah 58:6-9

Fasting will break the yoke of addiction and the connecting bonds of every other problem that has been feeding the addiction such as anxiety, depression and the nicotine dependency. It will undo the heavy burdens and start to heal you from the inside. Isaiah 58:6-9

Isaiah 58:6 "Is not this the kind of fasting I have chosen: to loose the chains of injustice and untie the cords of the yoke, to set the oppressed free and break every yoke?"

The flesh desires to live for and please itself, therefore fasting lowers our flesh while increasing our spiritual ability, strength, and awareness. It clarifies God's purpose in your situation as you become more open in the spirit. Fasting rekindles spiritual fire and builds faith. It helps to break Satan's power, resulting in deliverance and healing.

Isaiah 40:31; "But they that wait upon the LORD shall renew their strength; they shall mount up with wings as eagles; they shall run, and not be weary; and they shall walk, and not faint."

BEFORE YOU FAST: If you have any health concerns, consult your doctor before beginning your fast. If you have a health condition, are pregnant, or are taking medication, BE SAFE whatever you do.

How to operate Biblical Fasting.

Regulations to follow:

1. Fasting requires an intimate relationship with God, seeking His face in prayer, as well as abstaining from food and drink.
2. If you're fasting for longer than three days, you should drink water. Water should be clean, warm, and adequate.
3. The duration of a fast should be covenant between you and God, and the aim should be obvious; otherwise, the fast may be a waste of time, a hunger strike, or dieting.
4. If you want to perform strenuous chores or travel long distances, alternative liquids are recommended.
5. Avoid sexual interactions when fasting. I Cor.7:5

6. Throughout the fast, continue to pray and meditate on God's word. Listen for the Holy Spirit.

7. Remain disciplined and cautious when breaking the fast after the allotted number of days has passed. To avoid compromising your health, exercise more self-control over food.

1. Prayer: Harnessing the Power of Prayer.

Mark 9:28-29 "28 And when he was come into the house, his disciples asked him privately, why could not we cast him out? 29 And he said unto them, this kind can come forth by nothing, but by prayer and fasting."

One definition of prayer is divine dialogue or relationship with God. It's a conversation as you wait to hear from God.

Philippians 4:6-7 "6 Do not be anxious about anything, but in every situation, by prayer and petition, with thanksgiving, present your requests to God. 7 And the peace of God, which transcends all understanding, will guard your hearts and your minds in Christ Jesus."

Why we need prayers:

1. For God's ability to handle day-to-day tasks and to formulate the appropriate response to hardships.
2. To emulate Jesus.

1. For the ability to overcome in God's strength.
2. To ascertain God's will in every circumstance that arises.

Couple your fasting with prayer to God. Arrange time each day for 1 hour or more for daily prayer to God. To help you during prayer time, write down some prayer points and use them. Thank God for releasing you from the chains of addiction. Ask Him to reinforce your resolve to give up smoking.

Colossians 4:2- "Continue steadfastly in prayer, being watchful in it with thanksgiving."

The role of prayer in overcoming smoking addiction is of significant importance. Prayer serves as a powerful tool for seeking guidance, strength, and comfort during the quitting process. It allows individuals to tap into a higher power, finding solace and support on their journey towards breaking free from the chains of smoking addiction.

In addition to addressing physical cravings and psychological triggers, prayer helps individuals overcome spiritual barriers and doubts that may arise during the quitting process. It provides a space for surrendering addiction to God, seeking forgiveness, and finding restoration. Through prayer, individuals can experience a sense of liberation from guilt, shame, or unworthiness associated with addiction, embracing the truth that they are loved and supported by a God.

Moreover, prayer serves as a tool for emotional healing and resilience. It enables individuals to release negative emotions and find comfort during moments of temptation or vulnerability. By incorporating prayer into stress management techniques, emotional regulation practices, and seeking inner peace, individuals can cultivate emotional well-being while navigating the challenges of quitting smoking.

It is essential for readers to remember that their worth and identity are not defined by their addiction. In prayer, they can affirm their true identity as beloved children of God, deserving of love, acceptance, and a life free from the chains of smoking addiction.

Bible Reading and Prayers

Take a moment to read these bible verses, meditate on them and pray.

Use Prayer and Scripture as Weapons

Psalm 119:11: "I have hidden your word in my heart that I might not sin against you."

The Bible is filled with promises of strength, peace, and victory that can help you resist the urge to smoke. Prayer and meditation on scripture renew your mind and help you focus on God rather than the addiction.

Action Point: Make prayer a daily habit, especially when cravings strike. Memorize scriptures that remind you of God's power to help you overcome smoking.

3. Complete surrender to God

Proverbs 3:5-6 "5 Trust in the Lord with all your heart and lean not on your own understanding; 6 in all your ways submit to him, and he will make your paths straight."

Faith in God provides strength and resilience. It gives people hope and a sense of purpose, as well as a guiding light during difficult times. Through faith, God reminds us that we are not alone in our troubles. Quitting smoking is not always simple, and there may be times when we are tempted to grab a cigarette or doubt our ability to succeed. However, through faith in God, he will give us the inner strength we need to overcome these temptations and carry on with our commitment to become smoke-free.

Acknowledging your sins and admitting to them is a necessary part of complete surrender. Truly, God will forgive and hear you. **Romans 3:23 "for all have sinned and fall short of the glory of God"**. Ask God for pardon and mercy, as well as the divine ability to forsake your sins. Finally, ask God to take charge from this point forward. **Psalm 55:22 "Cast your burden on the Lord, And He shall sustain you; He shall never permit the righteous to be moved."**

Surrendering to God is important because sincere submission produces desirable spiritual fruit. **Galatians 5:24 "24 And they that are Christ's have crucified the flesh with the affections and lusts."**

By submitting to God, you allow Him to remove your nicotine addiction and cure you from within. There will be no more suffering; instead, you will experience excitement and peace. No more anxiety, stress, or disappointment over another failed attempt. You will think about a cigarette and meet individuals who smoke, but you will not be bothered or crave one. You are finally free. What appeared to be a mountain from afar is actually simply a little hill.

Bible Reading and Prayers

Take a moment to read these bible verses, meditate on them and pray.

Surrender Your Addiction to God

Matthew 11:28-30: "Come to me, all you who are weary and burdened, and I will give you rest."

Quitting smoking requires a surrender of your habit to God. Recognize that you cannot overcome it by your own strength but need God's help. Surrendering means asking God to help you every step of the way.

Philippians 4:13: "I can do all things through Christ who strengthens me."

Prayer Point: Pray and give your struggle with smoking to God. Ask Him to take control and give you the strength to prevail over it. Be open to letting go of habits that separate you from His best for your life.

4. Praise and Worship

Psalms 150:4: "praise him with timbrel and dancing, praise him with the strings and pipe"

Praise and worship are integral acts of devotion that express love, adoration, and reverence to God. Praise and worship strengthen your spiritual relationship to God, fostering mental tranquility, joy, and physical health. Regular worship can lead to transformation, greater faith, and a more fulfilling, Christ-centered life. God is pleased with us when we praise and worship Him, and He grants our requests in Jesus' name, Amen. Here's how you can express heartfelt praise and worship to God:

Praise through Song and Music- Music has long been a powerful way to glorify God. The Bible frequently encourages believers to sing and make music to the Lord. **Psalm 95:1-2: "1 Come, let us sing for joy to the Lord; let us shout aloud to the Rock of our salvation. 2 Let us come before him with thanksgiving and extol him with music and song."** And **Ephesians 5:19-20: "Speak to one another with psalms, hymns, and spiritual songs. Sing and make music in your heart to the Lord, always giving thanks to God the Father for everything, in the name of our Lord Jesus Christ."**

Use praise and worship songs to reflect on God's goodness, like singing popular songs such as "How Great is Our God" or "Here I Am to Worship." These songs draw attention to God's greatness, love, and sovereignty.

Worship through Prayer and Thanksgiving- Offering prayers of appreciation is a profound kind of worship. You can give earnest appreciation to God for His blessings, wisdom, and the gift of salvation. **1 Thessalonians 5:16-18: "16 Rejoice always, 17 pray without ceasing, 18 In everything give thanks: for this is the will of God in Christ Jesus concerning you."** Worship through prayer includes acknowledging God's greatness, confessing any sins, and expressing dependence on His power and love. A prayerful attitude keeps you aligned with God's will and in constant communication with Him.

Worship through Service- True worship entails living a life that reflects God's love and helping others. Worship goes beyond songs and prayers to include actions of charity, humility, and love. Find a way to serve God if you haven't already. Participate wholeheartedly in evangelism or one of the numerous projects in your church or community that support God's purpose for us and you will experience miracles in your life. **Romans 12:1: "Therefore, I urge you, brothers and sisters, in view of God's mercy, to offer your bodies as a living sacrifice, holy and pleasing to God—this is your true and proper worship."**

Praise God for His attributes and magnify God for who He is. Love: "God is love" 1 John 4:8. Holiness, "Holy, holy, holy is the Lord God Almighty" Revelation 4:8 and Faithfulness: "Great is Your faithfulness" Lamentations 3:23.

Spiritual strength comes through worship and often leads to divine intervention and victory over life's challenges. The Bible contains many examples where praising God led to supernatural breakthroughs. 2 Chronicles 20:22: When the people of Judah praised God, He set ambushes against their foes, resulting in victory without the need to battle. Acts 16:25-26: While imprisoned, Paul and Silas worshiped God, which resulted in a miracle earthquake that set them free.

5. Bible Study

Reading and meditating on God's scripture is very important and helpful in your journey freedom. The Bible reveals God's nature, His promises, and His works, which inspire deeper reverence. **Psalm 119:105: "Your word is a lamp to my feet and a light to my path."** By spending time studying the scriptures, you honor God's wisdom and guidance. Reflecting on verses that speak of His majesty and grace can deepen your worship experience.

Bible study can be a powerful support for those quitting smoking, providing encouragement, strength, and wisdom. **Philippians 4:13** reminds us, **"I can do all things through Christ who strengthens me,"** encouraging resilience through God's strength when facing the challenges of addiction Furthermore, 1 Corinthians 6:19-20 highlights the importance of treating the body as a temple of the Holy Spirit, encouraging a dedication to health and well-being as a means of honoring God.

Meditating on God's word and internalizing such scriptures can provide lasting encouragement, helping individuals find comfort, perseverance, and purpose on the path to freedom from smoking.

Now that you've learned about and understood the five essential strategies for breaking free from smoking addiction, you may begin your path to freedom. Recognize that your faith is a powerful weapon for overcoming challenges. By drawing inspiration from the testimonies and success stories of others who have found liberation through their faith, we can strengthen our resolve and cultivate the mindset needed for lasting change.

Psalm 91:14-15: "Because he loves me, says the Lord, I will rescue him; I will protect him, for he acknowledges my name."

Other important requirements to conquer your addiction.

1. You have to have faith because without faith it is impossible to please God. Hebrews 11:6
2. You need to be bold in your quest to break the bonds of addiction when you approach God's throne. Heb.4:16
3. In front of the Lord, humble yourself. God will exalt you if you sincerely yield to Him and acknowledge your sinfulness. Luke.18:10-21

Chapter 4

Understanding Smoking Addiction: The Physical and Psychological Effects

Proverbs 4:7 "Wisdom is the principal thing; therefore, get wisdom: and with all thy getting get understanding."

Nicotine disrupts the brain's reward system by increasing the release of dopamine, a neurotransmitter associated with pleasure and reward. This creates a sense of euphoria and reinforces smoking behaviors. Over time, the brain becomes dependent on nicotine to maintain normal functioning, leading to cravings and withdrawal symptoms while attempting to quit.

Smoking addiction has profound physical and psychological consequences, driven primarily by nicotine, the addictive chemical in tobacco. Understanding its effects is critical for overcoming smoking addiction.

Physical Effects:

1. **Lung and Heart Damage:** Smoking causes chronic lung diseases like COPD (chronic obstructive pulmonary disease), emphysema, and lung cancer. It also increases the risk of cardiovascular disease, stroke, and hypertension.

2. **Weakened Immune System:** Smokers are more susceptible to infections and have slower wound healing due to a compromised immune system. Smoking also damages the liver, kidneys, and digestive system, increasing the likelihood of liver disease, kidney failure, and gastrointestinal disorders.

3. **Cancer Risk:** Smoking is linked to various cancers, including lung, throat, mouth, and esophageal cancer.

4. **Respiratory Issues:** Chronic coughing, wheezing, and

shortness of breath are caused by damage to the airways and lung tissue by smoking.

5. **Addiction and Withdrawal Symptoms:** Nicotine causes dependency, and when smokers attempt to quit, they endure physical withdrawal symptoms such as headaches, restlessness, and an increased appetite. Source - journals.plos.org

Jeremiah 17:14: "Heal me, Lord, and I will be healed; save me and I will be saved, for you are the one I praise."

Prayer Point: Pray to God to restore your body and undo the damage caused by smoking.

Jeremiah 30:17: But I will restore you to health and heal your wounds,' declares the LORD, 'because you are called an outcast, Zion for whom no one cares.'

Psychological Effects:

1. **Nicotine Dependence:** Smoking addiction is rooted in nicotine's ability to stimulate dopamine release, providing a momentary sense of pleasure or relief, which reinforces the smoking habit.

2. **Stress and Anxiety:** Although many believe smoking helps manage stress, research shows it actually exacerbates anxiety over time. Withdrawal symptoms can heighten stress levels, creating a cycle where smokers need to light up to reduce the discomfort of withdrawal. Source - BMC Public Health. Philippians 4:6–7

3. **Mood Alterations:** Smokers often report irritability, frustration, and mood swings when they attempt to quit smoking, which can make it harder to quit successfully.

4. **Depression and Sense of Loss:** How to combat these feelings?

5. **Cognitive Impact:** Long-term smoking may affect memory,

cognitive function, and increase the risk of neurodegenerative diseases like Alzheimer's.

2 Timothy 1:7 "For the Spirit God gave us does not make us timid, but gives us power, love, and self-discipline."

Other Possible Effects:

1. **Headaches:** Headaches are another symptom that can occur during nicotine withdrawal. Staying hydrated by drinking enough of water throughout the day is essential for headache relief. Over-the-counter pain medications can also provide temporary relief.

1. **Insomnia or difficulty sleeping:** This could occur as the body adjusts to life without nicotine. Creating a relaxing bedtime routine can assist communicate to the body that it's time to unwind. Avoiding caffeine and electronic gadgets before bedtime, maintaining a comfortable sleep environment, and practicing relaxation techniques can promote better sleep.

Prayer Point: You should pray to God not to suffer any of these negative effects. Name each symptom and cancel it in the name of Jesus.

Romans 8:38–39 "38 For I am convinced that neither death nor life, neither angels nor demons, neither the present nor the future, nor any powers, 39 neither height nor depth, nor anything else in all creation, will be able to separate us from the love of God that is in Christ Jesus our Lord."

It is important to remember that the duration and severity of these symptoms will vary among individuals. Some may experience minimal discomfort, while others may face more intense challenges. Patience and self-compassion are key during this process.

Finally, smoking addiction causes significant physical harm to the body, particularly the lungs and heart, as well as trapping people in a cycle of psychological reliance, stress, and mood disorders.

In addition to the impact on the brain, smoking has serious bodily implications. Short-term consequences include an accelerated heart rate, high blood pressure, and constricted blood vessels. These immediate alterations can put a strain on the cardiovascular system, leading to long-term health issues like heart disease, stroke, and peripheral artery disease.

Recognizing the addictive qualities of smoking and its effects on mental and physical health allows you to gather the necessary information and support to overcome the addiction. To achieve freedom from smoking, you must have faith, follow the steps in this book, be determined, seek professional help when necessary, and you can add your own strategies to fit your needs.

2 Peter 1:5-7 "5 For this very reason, make every effort to add to your faith goodness; and to goodness, knowledge; 6 and to knowledge, self-control; and to self-control, perseverance; and to perseverance, godliness; 7 and to godliness, mutual affection; and to mutual affection, love."

Bible Reading and Prayers

Take a moment to read these bible verses, meditate on them and pray.

Seek Support from a Faith Community

Ecclesiastes 4:9-10: "Two are better than one... If either of them falls down, one can help the other up."

Discovering yourself in God and overcoming smoking becomes easier when you have support. Fellowship with other believers who can encourage, pray for, and hold you accountable is essential. It is entirely optional to disclose your addiction to anyone. With time, you will be able to do what feels right at each phase.

Prayer Point: Ask God to facilitate divine encounters with individuals and communities that will assist you on your path to victory. You can join a small group, talk to a mentor, or even seek professional counseling that combines faith and health if you like.

Chapter 5
The Power of Faith: Tapping into Divine Strength

Luke 1:37 "For with God nothing shall be impossible."

Action Point: As you read this chapter, reflect on the role your faith has played in your life so far and what God has done for you. Count your blessings one by one. Taking time each day to pause, reflect, and communicate with God can help cultivate a sense of peace and clarity. Whether it's in the morning, before meals, or before bed, finding a consistent prayer practice that works for you can provide a foundation of faith and determination.

2 Corinthians 5:7 "For we live by faith, not by sight."

Faith Over Habit: A Biblical Path to Freedom from Smoking demonstrates how faith is an effective aid in the struggle to quit smoking. God brings peace and direction throughout the quitting process. By placing your trust in Him, you can use your faith to gain strength and drive when faced with challenges. Many people have found consolation and inspiration in God, enabling them to persevere during terrible circumstances.

We read in the Bible about Job, and it demonstrates the strength of perseverance in the face of adversity. Job faced severe hardship but stayed loyal in his faith, eventually achieving restoration and healing. **James 5:11 "Behold, we count them happy which endure. Ye have heard of the patience of Job, and have seen the end of the Lord; that the Lord is very pitiful, and of tender mercy."**

Similarly, Joseph's narrative highlights the value of persistence and tenacity, as he survived treachery and jail to achieve his goal. Genesis 37:1-36.

The account of David and Goliath. David, a youthful shepherd, confronted an apparently insurmountable foe in the terrifying Goliath.

Despite the odds stacked against him, David used his faith in God to defeat Goliath with a single stone. 1 Samuel 17. Moses is another inspirational biblical figure. When faced with the task of leading the Israelites out of Egypt, Moses encountered numerous obstacles along the way. Through faith and perseverance, Moses successfully led his people to freedom. Hebrews 11: **Faith in Action**. However, he stayed steadfast in his faith, confident that God would guide him.

These stories tell us that no difficulty is too great when we put our faith in God. With unshakeable faith, we can overcome any barrier that comes our way. Applying these principles to the road of quitting smoking entails drawing on your inner strength, driven by faith, to remain dedicated to your objective of quitting smoking even when cravings or temptations emerge.

With faith on your side, you will achieve positive results. After quitting smoking, I felt better physically and emotionally, and food never tasted better. My life no longer revolves on my next cigarette. I no longer have to race to my enslaver; I am finally free of this twilight zone. It had always bothered me that I could quit or change undesirable behaviors, but smoking was extremely difficult. No matter what I tried, yet once I introduced God and let Him take over, everything fell into place. I experienced no negative side effects, such as headaches or withdrawal symptoms, after stopping smoking. I removed all traces of cigarettes from my home, and I didn't miss or crave them. It felt as if I had never smoked before; the only reminder was the significant health improvements taking place in my body. I could breathe easier.

Chapter 6

Renewing the Mind: Cultivating a Smoke-Free Mentality

Brain Rehabilitation

Psalm 139:13 "For you created my inmost being; you knit me together in my mother's womb."

When brain cells are injured and die from a brain aneurysm or a stroke owing to a lack of oxygen, they do not proliferate. So, brain rehabilitation is used to help establish new neural pathways that repair or improve cognitive and functional abilities, akin to rerouting signals in the brain to bypass damaged areas or optimize performance.

When you smoke, nicotine activates dopaminergic (DAergic) neurons in the ventral tegmental area (VTA) of the brain's mesocorticolimbic reward circuitry. The release of dopamine into the brain, combined with recurrent nicotine use, creates a pathway that leads to addiction. Article from the National Library of Medicine. To escape the smoking addiction cycle, one must go through brain rehabilitation, which is critical for developing healthy pathways.

You have tried and failed multiple times to give up smoking. You now think it's impossible since it's turned into a cycle, but God made it possible. Rewiring your brain, also known as neuroplasticity, refers to the brain's ability to reorganize itself by forming new neural connections throughout life. This process allows your brain to adapt, learn new things, and recover from injury.

Understanding Neuroplasticity

The brain was once thought to be static, with fixed pathways. However, research in the past few decades has shown that the brain is highly adaptable. Neuroplasticity is driven by behaviors, experiences, learning, and even thoughts. Key studies from neuroscientists like Dr. Michael Merzenich have shown that our brains can be "retrained" through repeated behaviors and experiences.

Romans 12:2 "Do not conform to the pattern of this world, but be transformed by the renewing of your mind. Then you will be able to test and approve what God's will is—His good, pleasing and perfect will."

The mind plays a crucial role in the journey towards breaking free from smoking addiction. Our thoughts and beliefs have a powerful influence on our behavior, including our smoking habits. Neuroplasticity is a mechanism that can be leveraged to quit smoking by breaking old neural pathways tied to smoking habits and forming new, healthier ones. Psalm 1:2 says "Instead, they find happiness in the Teaching of the Lord, and they think about it day and night". Find satisfaction in the Lord and give Him priority in your life. To encourage brain rewiring, read God's word, pray, fast, and exercise. With these new behaviors, you can make long-term adjustments and successfully quit smoking.

In no time your brain will create new pathways that are healthy and confident without the use of nicotine or any substitutes. Negative thought patterns that often hold you back from making positive changes in your live. Thoughts like "I can't quit" or "I need cigarettes to cope" no longer create barriers to your success. You can now recognize these negative thoughts and repeatedly rewire them using the tools you have learned in Faith over habit: A biblical Path to Freedom. You now understand and belief that cigarettes were never and are not necessary for coping with stress or difficult emotions. You now handle stressful situations and all challenges with ease and with God by your side.

You do not worry about thoughts of smoking because you understand they are just thoughts just like any other and you do not have to act on them. You do not fear or worry about smoking because that is no longer you. You fully understand that smoking does not positively contribute to your life but only steal time, rob and destroy you. You are no longer a slave but in control.

Chapter 7

Free from the Bondage: Breaking the chains of illusions.

Now that you have, by the grace of God, surrendered to God, you must now learn to live and operate successfully in your new home. This is necessary because the devil is watching. 1 Peter 5:8 "Be alert and of sober mind. Your enemy the devil prowls around like a roaring lion looking for someone to devour." He is not pleased with your decision to quit smoking since he knows that this addiction causes various types of illnesses, anxiety, and suffering in your life. He wants to kill you spiritually and physically; therefore, Satan does not give up simply; he works hard to reclaim us.

Satan will employ several ways to destroy us, including being subtle. **Genesis.3:1 "Now the serpent was more subtle than any beast of the field which the LORD God had made. And he said unto the woman, Yea, hath God said, Ye shall not eat of every tree of the garden?".** Do not make the mistake of thinking that one puff or one cigarette is harmless; that is the Devil's sweet spot, and it's always a downward path from there.

Deception: - Revelations 12:9 "So the great dragon was cast out, that serpent of old, called the Devil and Satan, who deceives the whole world; he was cast to the earth, and his angels were cast out with him". Many individuals, including myself, fell into the trap of believing that e-cigarettes, lights/low-tar, or oral tobacco are less harmful than cigarettes, but research and advice has indicated that they too, come with their own set of health issues. Tobacco use in any form raises your risk of developing significant health problems such as diabetes and cancer. Some people use nicotine replacement therapy, such as nicotine gum and patches, to facilitate their transition to nonsmoking. NRT still contains nicotine, the primary active component in tobacco products.

According to studies, it may not create major health problems, but because it is addictive, it will most likely prolong and reinforce individual tobacco addiction behavior.

Nicotine is addictive, and people can shift their dependency from tobacco to nicotine replacements. Do you realize the irony here? Using nicotine to treat a nicotine addiction is similar to treating obesity with junk food. Quitting smoking entails not just removing nicotine from your body, but also unplugging the rituals linked with your pre-smoke and post-smoke experiences. You might enjoy your cigarette with a cup of coffee and another before leaving the house. All of these rituals and the nicotine itself have to be eliminated simultaneously in order to completely break the addiction.

Tempter: - Matthew 4:1 **"Then Jesus was led up by the Spirit into the wilderness to be tempted by the devil".** At your most vulnerable, the Devil may appear powerful, incessantly whispering the numerous reasons why you should smoke again and constantly displaying proof of your previous attempts to live an addiction-free life in order to undermine your confidence. This is the time to remember that the Devil has limitations; he lacks God's 'omni' attributes, so he is only smoke and mirrors. The Bible instructs us to combat the devil with the word of God and to give him no place in our life. We must fully understand his tactics in order to successfully counter and frustrate his attempts to influence us.

Breaking free from chains of addiction involves aligning your spiritual growth with God's strength, wisdom, and guidance. Only then will you be able to recognize the Devil's traps and illusions that keep you bound, but because you drew near to God, you will become stronger to overcome and break destructive habits. Galatians 5:1

Bible Reading and Prayers

Take a moment to read these bible verses, meditate on them and pray.

Depend on the Holy Spirit's Power.

Galatians 5:16: "So I say, walk by the Spirit, and you will not gratify the desires of the flesh."

The Holy Spirit empowers you to overcome habits that are harmful to your body and spirit. Ask the Holy Spirit to help you fight against cravings, manage stress, and develop healthier ways of living.

2 Timothy 1:7: "For God has not given us a spirit of fear, but of power and of love and of a sound mind."

Pray Point: Before each day begins, ask the Holy Spirit to guide and strengthen you. Acknowledge that quitting smoking is not just a physical battle but a spiritual one where God's Spirit can give you victory.

Chapter 8

Coping with Triggers and Temptations: Strategies for Emotional Resilience

Ephesians 6:13 "Therefore put on the full armor of God, so that when the day of evil comes, you may be able to stand your ground, and after you have done everything, to stand."

Quitting smoking is a challenging journey that comes with its fair share of obstacles and setbacks. It's crucial to acknowledge the potential challenges and triggers that may arise along the way in order to effectively navigate them and stay committed to your goal of becoming smoke-free.

Some common challenges faced by many individuals attempting to quit smoking

Stress:

Matthew 11:28-30: "28 Come to me, all you who are weary and burdened, and I will give you rest. 29 Take my yoke upon you and learn from me, for I am gentle and humble in heart, and you will find rest for your souls. 30 For my yoke is easy and my burden is light."

Stressful situations frequently lead to an increased need for cigarettes as a coping mechanism. Unfortunately, we cannot avoid terrible situations in life, but we can learn to deal with them through Christ. Because nicotine delivers an immediate sense of relaxation, some smokers believe, or have been indoctrinated to believe, that it relieves stress and anxiety. It is crucial to recognize your stressors so you are prepared to deal with them accordingly in a healthy manner and slowly dissociate your stressors with cigarettes. Remember that cigarettes will not help you relax; they are merely a clutch, and studies have shown that smoking increases anxiety and tension.

According to Truth Initiative.org, tobacco companies have a long history of promoting cigarettes as stress relievers, and the World Health Organization (WHO) reports that the tobacco industry is now targeting young people by marketing tobacco and nicotine products as less harmful novel products, such as gadgets or toys, in attractive packaging. Highlight Office 4 by Focol Vape and Penjamin Vape Cart Pens by Delta 8 Resellers are two examples of vape brands that offer them as school supplies. Evidence suggests that these products, available in fruit and candy tastes and highly pushed on social media platforms, are enticing young people all over the world into smoking.

The American Cancer Society states that smoking is damaging to teenagers' brain development. Smoking may provide a brief sense of relaxation, but the body's stress level will rapidly rise. Your blood pressure and pulse rate will increase, your muscles will constrict, and less oxygen will be accessible to your body and brain. Tobacco and nicotine products, in any form, are extremely addictive and have a high risk of cardiovascular and respiratory disorders, as well as death.

When you are on your quitting journey and encounter a stressful situation, avoid smoking because starting again only replenishes the nicotine in your system and restarts the process, thus it is preferable to address the source of the stressful event. Furthermore, a study published in PLOS ONE indicated that smokers who believe smoking relieves stress are less motivated to quit and had worse success rates with cessation attempts. Those who successfully quit smoking, on the other hand, report considerable reductions in stress and anxiety.

Most people started smoking in their teens because they were curious, wanted to look cool, or wanted to fit in with their peers. Nobody ever said, "I will learn to smoke to relieve stress." The smoking procedure is stressful; it involves a lot of coughing, whizzing, dizziness, and most likely vomiting due to the horrible taste of nicotine and your body's rejection of this foreign chemical. It is not until we become hooked that our brain begins to correlate smoking with stress. Yet, we overlook the fact that prior to the addiction, all smokers faced and handled stressful events successfully without the need of a cigarette.

The good news is that the belief that cigarettes ease stress is simply a brainwashing marketing ploy devised by tobacco firms. YouTube reviews, catchy lines, smoking cowboys, and attractive beach ladies have all contributed to promote the concept. Psalms 10:7. The light at the end of the tunnel is that you can deal with stressful situations without using nicotine. Your physical form is a marvelous design crafted by our God, complete with all the tools needed to navigate life's challenges.

Prayer point: Thank the Lord for his love and ask Him to make your road easy and relieve your anxiety, tension, and stress and replace them with peace, joy, and love.

Emotional distress:

Matthew 7:13-14 "13 Enter through the narrow gate. For wide is the gate and broad is the road that leads to destruction, and many enter through it. 14 But small is the gate and narrow the road that leads to life, and only a few find it.

Emotional distress is another factor that can contribute to relapse during the quitting process. Feelings of sadness, anxiety, or frustration may tempt you to turn to smoking as a way to cope. Recognizing these emotions and finding healthy outlets for them is crucial. Engaging in praise and worship, prayer walk or bible reading activities will bring you joy and provide emotional release. Be proud of your courage in conquering this addiction. **Romans 3: 3- 5 "3 Not only so, but we also glory in our sufferings, because we know that suffering produces perseverance; 4 perseverance, character; and character, hope. 5 And hope does not put us to shame, because God's love has been poured out into our hearts through the Holy Spirit, who has been given to us."**

Be Kind and Loving to yourself:

Self-compassion is an effective approach to regulate your emotions. We're too hard on ourselves. Quitting smoking can be difficult, so be kind to yourself throughout the process. Treating oneself with care and empathy will help you deal with unpleasant emotions without turning to smoking. Reminding yourself that setbacks are a natural part of the process and being gentle with yourself will help you build emotional resilience.

Being kind and loving to yourself is essential for nurturing your well-being and living in harmony with God's purpose for your life. Treat yourself with grace. Embrace self-care, rest, and forgiveness as acts of love. **Psalm 139:14**, says, **"I praise you, for I am fearfully and wonderfully made. Wonderful are your works; my soul knows it very well".** Acknowledge your worth as God's creation. Additionally, Jesus teaches us to love one another in **Mark 12:31 "The second is this: Love your neighbor as yourself. There is no commandment greater than these,"** reminding us that self-love is foundational to loving others. By showing yourself kindness, you reflect the love God has for you.

Galatians 6:9 "Do not grow weary in doing good, for at the proper time you will reap a harvest if you do not give up."

Be gentle with yourself while you quit smoking, recognizing that each stride forward represents progress. Celebrate small victories, and remember that God's grace is sufficient. Lean on His strength, as **Philippians 4:13** reminds us, **"I can do all things through Christ who strengthens me."**

Dealing with Trauma:

Psalms 34:18 "The LORD is close to the brokenhearted and saves those who are crushed in spirit."

If you have any unresolved trauma or mental health issue, such as anxiety, it will be incredibly beneficial to address the trauma or disorder as part of your smoking cessation efforts. Because if you suffer from anxiety and use cigarettes as a coping mechanism, quitting will be difficult owing to your subconscious perception that cigarettes relieve anxiety. Despite the fact that smoking exacerbates the problem. Seeking professional counseling or therapy, preferably from a certified therapist with a Christian background, will help you cope with your trauma and further your efforts to quit smoking. A qualified therapist with a Christian background can provide professional guidance and spiritual support tailored to each individual's specific requirements to build emotional resilience. Seek adequate treatment for mental health disorders. Emphasizing that seeking professional help is not a sign of weakness but rather a sign of strength and commitment to one's well-being is essential.

Joseph's narrative is a striking biblical example of trauma. Joseph was sold into slavery by his brothers in Genesis 37, and then imprisoned in Genesis 39, after being falsely accused of rape by Potiphar's wife. Despite these traumatic events, Joseph remained steadfast in his faith, eventually experiencing redemption and reaching greatness.

Leaning on God is essential to overcoming traumatic situations and staying committed to quitting smoking. **Philippians 4:13 "I can do all this through him who gives me strength."**

Action step: Pause for a moment and envision how your life will be enhanced after smoking no longer holds power over you. You will experience improved health, increased vitality, and stronger relationships with loved ones who have been harmed by your addiction. By focusing on these positive outcomes, you will boost your motivation to overcome any hurdles that arise.

Bible Reading and Prayers

Take a moment to read these bible verses, meditate on them and pray.

Identify and Replace Triggers with Positive Habits

1 Corinthians 10:13: "No temptation has overtaken you except what is common to mankind. And God is faithful; He will not let you be tempted beyond what you can bear."

Smoking is often linked to triggers like stress, boredom, or social situations. To quit smoking, recognize these triggers and replace them with healthy, God-honoring habits.

Action Point: Identify the situations or emotions that trigger your urge to smoke. Replace these moments with prayer, exercise, or spending time in worship. Let your dependence shift from cigarettes to God. One good example of a God-honoring habit is a prayer walk. A prayer walk is a spiritual practice that combines walking and praying. In this situation, the stroll will serve as both your daily workout and your prayer time. There are various power walking or speed walking strategies, and you can select the one that best suits you. I prefer the brisk walk because the pace keeps me in the moment, in sync with my prayers, attentive, and able to pray without becoming winded.

This style of walk is typically completed at a relatively fast pace, faster than your ordinary walking pace. Through devotion to God, your spiritual life will begin to improve, as will your physical body as you begin to exercise and recover from addiction.

Chapter 9

Overcoming Obstacles: Navigating Social Pressures and Peer Influence

1 Corinthians 15:33 "Do not be deceived: "Bad company ruins good morals."

Social interactions can also present substantial challenges for persons attempting to quit smoking. Being around smokers, or attending activities where smoking is widespread, might create temptation and make it difficult to resist the impulse to light up. These triggers can include witnessing other people smoke, feeling pressured to fit in, or associating smoking with specific activities or settings. Social interactions that could lead to relapse should be minimized or canceled in the beginning, especially if your absence has no impact on the occasion.

1 Corinthians 10:13 "No temptation has overtaken you except what is common to mankind. And God is faithful; he will not let you be tempted beyond what you can bear. But when you are tempted, he will also provide a way out so that you can endure it."

If you cannot avoid smokers, whether at work or at home, it's crucial to have exit measures in place to help you avoid being tempted to smoke.

Setting boundaries is a useful strategy. Clearly communicate your decision to quit smoking to your friends and acquaintances. Inform them that you would appreciate their support and understanding throughout this process. Setting these boundaries helps to create a supportive environment that is aligned with your objectives.

Avoid smoking areas and instead use the opportunity to spend time with God if you are at work.

You can find supportive relationships in the church community. This can provide vital direction and a sense of belonging as you navigate the obstacles of social situations. Matthew 7:7-8

Dealing with peer pressure needs assertiveness and self-assurance. Remind yourself of your dedication and the reasons for your decision to quit smoking. Assertiveness in social situations will reinforce your determination and help you stick to your goals.

Maintaining your values in social situations is critical to long-term success in overcoming smoking addiction. Draw inspiration from biblical stories and teachings that emphasize the necessity of acting in accordance with one's convictions. Remember that quitting smoking is a personal decision, so be steadfast in your resolve. Express your needs and desires without feeling guilty or sorry about your decision.

4 strategies to help you set effective boundaries

Proverbs 13:20 "He that walketh with wise men shall be wise: but a companion of fools shall be destroyed."

1. When offered a cigarette, express explicitly your decision to quit smoking.
2. Establish non-negotiables: For example, you may decide not to attend smoking-friendly events or gatherings until you are more confident in avoiding triggers.
3. Practice saying "NO" by politely and firmly declining offers of smokes. Avoid being defensive or feeling compelled to justify your decisions.
4. Surround yourself with supportive people. Seek out partnerships that support your decision to quit smoking while respecting your boundaries.

1 Corinthians 15:33 "Do not be misled: "Bad company corrupts good character."

Prayer Point: Ask God for the courage to resist the temptation to smoke and to decline offers to smoke when you go out into the world.

Chapter 10
Building Healthy Habits: Positive Lifestyle

Matthew 6:33 "But seek first his kingdom and his righteousness, and all these things will be given to you as well."

Now that you have learned how to develop and implement healthy spiritual habits like prayer, bible reading, worship, and fasting, it's time to look into healthy living habits to supplement what you have learned in this book. These new behaviors should integrate easily without feeling burdensome or forced, thereby contributing fully to your total well-being.

The benefit of stopping smoking is that your body will begin to mend. Nicotine is leaving your body, and you no longer feel lethargic and nauseous all the time. You also have more energy. The biggest blessing is that you are no longer a slave to nicotine. Nicotine is no longer stealing your time that could be spent on essential things like family, and it is no longer shortening your life or the lives of those around you. You have regained your free will, just as God intended.

It is critical to swiftly use this free time and energy to establish healthy habits, as **"Idle hands are the devil's workshop; idle lips are his mouthpiece." Proverbs 16:27.** Furthermore, new habits, such as those indicated below, have been shown to assist your body heal from nicotine damage and eliminate nicotine from the system. Healthy and spiritual habits will benefit you physically, emotionally, mentally, and spiritually. You can create and change your habits as you see fit, and you can find further ideas on the internet.

Exercise: - is a powerful tool in your journey towards a smoke-free life. Engaging in regular physical activity can serve as a natural stress reliever and a healthy way to release tension. Whether it's going for a prayer walk, jogging, cycling, or participating in a fitness class, pick an exercise program that appeals to you and commit to it. it will also improve your physical health and boost your mood.

Nutrition: - is essential for quitting smoking addiction. Certain foods can help lower the desire to smoke and improve your overall health. Consider adding fruits, vegetables, whole grains, and lean protein to your diet. These nutrient-dense meals include critical vitamins, minerals, and antioxidants that benefit both physical and mental health. Furthermore, maintaining hydrated by drinking enough of water throughout the day might help eliminate toxins from your system. Cigarettes and greasy foods go together. Cigarettes can also help to decrease appetite. Genesis 1:29 "And God said, "Behold, I have given you every plant yielding seed that is on the face of all the earth, and every tree with seed in its fruit. You shall have them for food."

Giving back: - is another way to thank God for all He has done for you. Taking the opportunity to assist others and engage in activities that offer joy and honor to God can help you shift your focus away from smoking. Identify your passion in God's ministry and volunteer for it. This could involve singing in the choir, evangelizing, teaching Bible classes, painting, or other church-related charity work. The Bible states that giving offers greater satisfaction than receiving. **Acts 20:35-36 "In everything I did, I showed you that by this kind of hard work we must help the weak, remembering the words the Lord Jesus himself said: 'It is more blessed to give than to receive."**

Self-care: - techniques are another excellent strategy to break the habit of smoking. Taking time for yourself and participating in things that bring you joy and relaxation will help you shift your focus away from smoking. Explore hobbies or interests that you've always wanted to pursue but haven't had the time for. This could include music, prayer, writing, gardening, cooking, or any other activity that feeds your spirit. You can also have your teeth whitened. **Mark 1:35** Jesus Prays in a Solitary Place: **"Very early in the morning, while it was still dark,**

Jesus got up, left the house and went off to a solitary place, where he prayed."

Eat only when you truly need to eat to avoid making food your new addiction. Some people may gain some weight, which is quite normal. It's merely your healthy system kicking in after a lengthy period of suppressed appetite from nicotine.

By combining these healthy habits with your spiritual habits, you not only replace the smoking habit but also create a good lifestyle that promotes general well-being. Remember that developing healthy habits demands self-discipline and accountability. When developing new routines and goals, you must be patient with yourself. Be kind as you hold yourself accountable and stay diligent in your efforts; you will be able to overcome obstacles and remain inspired to choose healthier choices.

Chapter 11

Staying Committed: Maintaining Long-Term Success in Smoke-Free Living

6 Strategies to Help Prevent Relapse

2 Corinthians 3:17 "Now the Lord is the Spirit, and where the Spirit of the Lord is, there is freedom."

Preventing relapse is an important part of staying dedicated to quitting smoking and achieving long-term success in a smoke-free lifestyle. By implementing the practical advice and strategies in this book, you can improve your chances of being smoke-free. Identify triggers and seek support when needed. Here are some strategies to consider:

1. **Identify Triggers:** Recognizing situations, emotions, or activities that can trigger the desire to smoke is critical in avoiding a relapse. Stress, social circumstances, alcohol intake, and specific smoking-related locales or persons are all common triggers. Take a note of these triggers. Awareness is the first step in building effective methods. 2 Timothy 1:7

1. **Use the Key strategies:** Once you have identified your triggers, create prayers tailored to each situation, using the 5 key strategies for Breakthrough as a guide. Repeatedly pray for them, and fast when things get tough.

2. **Create a Support System:** Pray that God will help you surround yourself with supportive people who understand your journey and can offer encouragement and accountability, which is critical for preventing relapse. Remember, you do not have to go through this alone. John 16:33

3. **Seek Professional Help if Needed:** Do not hesitate to seek professional assistance when necessary. It could be spiritual, physical, or mental. Matthew 11:28

4. **Stay Mindful of Your Progress:** Regularly remind yourself of your progress since quitting smoking. Celebrate your accomplishments and milestones along the road. This positive reinforcement will help you maintain your commitment to a smoke-free lifestyle and provide encouragement during difficult moments.

5. **Accountability:** Hold yourself accountable when you make mistakes. Be firm but kind to yourself. Remember that relapse does not equal failure; it is merely a short setback. Use the situation to learn and adapt your strategies accordingly.

Stay dedicated, be patient with yourself, and believe in your capacity to live a smoke-free lifestyle. With perseverance and drive, you can overcome any obstacle that comes your way.

7 practical steps for creating a smoke-free environment:

1. **Let God take over:** Surrender everything to God and trust that He will see you through it all.

2. **Remove Smoking Paraphernalia:** Remove all cigarettes, lighters, ashtrays, and other smoking-related materials from your environment. This covers your house, car, office, and any other place where you spend a lot of time. Removing these smoking-related reminders will help lessen the temptation to relapse.

3. **Clean and Refresh Your Living Spaces:** Thoroughly clean your home and other living areas to remove any leftover odors

or residue from smoking. If feasible, wash the drapes, furniture, and bedding, as well as the carpets and walls. This will contribute to a fresh and clean environment that promotes your smoke-free lifestyle.

4. **Create Smoke-Free Zones:** Designate specific sections of your house or office as smoke-free. Inform your family, friends, and coworkers about your decision to quit smoking and ask for their help in preserving a smoke-free atmosphere. Setting clear boundaries will help prevent exposure to secondhand smoke and lessen the chance of cravings.

5. **Replace Smoking Habits with Healthy Alternatives:** Find healthier ways to deal with stress or boredom to avoid smoking sessions. Engage in activities or hobbies. Take a prayer walk or learn to cook.

6. **Establish New Routines:** Develop new daily routines that do not involve smoking and in places that do not allow smoking. Plan activities that get you excited to fill the time, such as exercising, bible reading, or attending prayer service. These positive and fulfilling activities, will reinforce your commitment to living a smoke-free life.

7. **Seek Support from Loved Ones:** Surrounding yourself with people who support your journey to quit smoking can be a source of encouragement and motivation.

Bible Reading and Prayers

Take a moment to read these bible verses, meditate on them and pray

Matthew 7:7 Ask, Seek, Knock "Ask and it will be given to you; seek and you will find; knock and the door will be opened to you."

Prayer Point: Ask God to help you create a smoke-free environment. Pray for perseverance and determination in your pursuit of freedom. By removing triggers and developing new habits and routines, you can create an environment that supports your desire to live a smoke-free life. Pray for strength, focus, and the restored freedom that comes with achieving long-term success in your quest to a smoke-free future.

Chapter 12
Looking Forward: A Life Transformed by Faith Over Habit.

Joshua 1:8-9 "8 Keep this Book of the Law always on your lips; meditate on it day and night, so that you may be careful to do everything written in it. Then you will be prosperous and successful. 9 Have I not commanded you? Be strong and courageous. Do not be afraid; do not be discouraged, for the Lord your God will be with you wherever you go."

Remember, recognizing and celebrating milestones achieved during the quitting process is crucial for motivation and commitment. These accomplishments build confidence and reinforce belief in overcoming smoking addiction.

Reflect on how faith has influenced your transformational journey, helping you overcome smoking addiction. Despite doubts, fear, and uncertainty, God consistently provides strength, comfort, and guidance. Additionally, your faith has offered solace during moments of withdrawal or cravings, giving the strength you needed to overcome these obstacles.

Countless people have found new joy, purpose, and fulfillment after successfully quitting smoking. Imagine waking up every morning feeling energized and healthy, free of tobacco's negative effects. You can easily engage in physical activities, thanks to your increased stamina and lung function. You are enjoying the benefits of a smoke-free lifestyle on your relationships since you are no longer concerned about exposing loved ones to secondhand smoke. Accept the freedom to completely enjoy social occasions, knowing that you are no longer trapped by the bonds of addiction.

Maintaining commitment and determination is essential for long-term success in living a smoke-free life. Challenges may arise, and temptations may appear along the path. However, with the tools and tactics you've learned throughout this book, you'll be able to overcome these challenges with confidence and elegance.

Finally, let me express gratitude for the journey you have embarked upon—the journey towards a life transformed by faith over habit. You have showed incredible courage and resilience so far, and as you continue on, keep your faith sturdy and your determination unshakable. Embrace all that lies ahead—a future filled with hope, purpose, and joy as you experience the freedom of a smoke-free life.

Romans 12: 1 "Therefore, I urge you, brothers and sisters, in view of God's mercy, to offer your bodies as a living sacrifice, holy and pleasing to God—this is your true and proper worship."

Here is a message of hope, gratitude, and inspiration

Psalm 37:23-24 "23 The Lord makes firm the steps of the one who delights in him; 24 though he may stumble, he will not fall, for the Lord upholds him with his hand."

I want to commend you on your progress and celebrate the transformation that has taken place in your life thus far. I am grateful that you have allowed God and me to be a part of your journey to overcome your smoking addiction. I encourage you to keep working on your goal of quitting smoking. Remember: you are not alone. The bible says, **Isaiah 41:10 "10 So do not fear, for I am with you; do not be dismayed, for I am your God. I will strengthen you and help you; I will uphold you with my righteous right hand."**

May you be guided by God. Staying connected to God provides you with a source of strength, comfort, and love. In challenging times, always reflect on how God has influenced your transformational journey thus far, and continue to draw on His power as you navigate the future. In times of doubt or difficulty, trust that God will offer the assistance you require to keep going forward.

Love and cherish yourself. Stay committed to your goal, persevere through any challenges that may come your way, and stay connected to God and your support system. With dedication and tenacity, you will continue to alter your life and experience the long-term benefits of a smoke-free lifestyle. I believe in you and that you can overcome your smoking addiction. May this incredible journey to freedom bring you strength, purpose, joy, and fulfillment.

Memory Verse: Psalm 139:13-14

Memorize these verses and believe that you are precious and extraordinary. God has a purpose for you.

"13 For you created my inmost being; you knit me together in my mother's womb.

14 I praise you because I am fearfully and wonderfully made; your works are wonderful; I know that full well."

Bible Reading and Prayers

Take a moment to read these bible verses, meditate on them and pray.

Celebrate Small Victories

Philippians 1:6: "Being confident of this, that He who began a good work in you will carry it on to completion until the day of Christ Jesus."

Every step toward quitting is a victory. Celebrate small milestones and remind yourself that through God's grace, you are moving forward.

Prayer Point: If you go a day, week, or month without smoking, give thanks to God. Praise Him for each small triumph, knowing He is working in you. Acts 16:25-26

Chapter 13
Prayer Points

Below are some model prayer points, specifically tailored to overcoming smoking addiction. You can add more points and couple them with Bible verses.

1. "I am free from the chains of smoking and living a healthier lifestyle. Every day, I am moving closer to a smoke-free life." Each day focus on aligning your thoughts with God's will for your life. Romans 12:2

2. "I am strong and capable of overcoming any cravings or triggers. I am in control of my actions and choose not to let smoking define me." Actively challenge and bind with prayer negative thoughts and beliefs associated with smoking addiction. 2 Corinthians 10:5

3. "My health and well-being are more important than the brief pleasure of smoking. Each fresh breath I take serves as a reminder of my dedication to a smoke-free lifestyle." 1 Corinthians 6:12

4. "I release any attachment to cigarettes and embrace my freedom with open arms. I am resilient and have the power to overcome any challenges along my journey." Anchor yourself in biblical principles, and tap into a source of strength beyond yourself. 2 Corinthians 3:17

5. "I am breaking free from the grip of addiction and embracing a brighter future. I choose to nourish my body with clean air and live a life full of vitality." Overcome your own limitations and doubts through trust in God's guidance, like Moses. The apostle Paul underwent a radical transformation from persecutor to follower of Christ, demonstrating the power of divine

intervention in changing hearts and minds. John 8:36

6. "Lord, grant me the strength to overcome every temptation to smoke, knowing that through You, I can conquer all things." Philippians 4:13

7. "Father, I commit my body to You as Your temple. Help me honor You by caring for it and rejecting habits that harm it." 1 Corinthians 6:19-20

8. "Jesus, thank You for the gift of new beginnings. May I step into each smoke-free day with hope and trust in Your guidance." 2 Corinthians 5:17

9. "Lord, help me renew my mind daily so that my thoughts align with Your truth, not the lies of addiction." Romans 12:2

10. "Father, remind me that Your grace is sufficient for me, especially in moments of weakness or cravings." 2 Corinthians 12:9

11. "Lord, I declare freedom in Your name! Break every chain of addiction that holds me captive and help me walk in victory." John 8:36

12. "Jesus, help me focus on Your goodness instead of fleeting desires. You are my ultimate source of joy and peace." Psalm 16:11

13. "God, fill my heart with a desire for health and wholeness, and let every craving for smoking fade away." Jeremiah 29:11

14. "Lord, guard my thoughts and actions so I choose life and health, knowing that each small decision honors You." Deuteronomy 30:19

15. "Father, I surrender my struggles and cravings to You. Replace my weaknesses with Your strength." Psalm 55:22

16. "Holy Spirit, guide me in seeking comfort and stress relief from You, not harmful substances like cigarettes." Matthew 11:28-30

17. "Lord, help me trust in Your timing and process. I believe that You will complete the good work You've started in me."

Philippians 1:6

18. "God, give me the courage to remove triggers and negative influences that lead me to smoke, trusting You with the change." Proverbs 3:5-6

19. "Jesus, teach me to care for myself as You care for me. Fill me with love and patience toward myself as I grow." Ephesians 5:29

20. "Lord, let my journey to quit smoking become a testimony of Your power, inspiring others to seek freedom in You." Revelation 12:11

Thanksgiving Prayer Points

1. "Lord, I thank You for the victory You have given me over smoking. Your strength has made my freedom possible." *1 Corinthians 15:57*

2. "Father, I am grateful for the health You are restoring to me and for the breath of life that fills my lungs anew." *Psalm 103:3-4*

3. "Thank You, Lord, for Your unending grace that sustained me through my journey to freedom. Without You, I would not have made it." *2 Corinthians 12:9*

4. "Jesus, I thank You for breaking the chains of addiction in my life and leading me into a new season of hope and healing." *Psalm 107:14*

5. "God, I thank You for replacing my cravings with a hunger for Your Word and Your presence in my life." *Matthew 5:6*

6. "Father, I praise You for being my refuge and my strength in moments of temptation and weakness." *Psalm 46:1*

7. "Thank You, Lord, for the community and support You've provided to encourage me on this journey." *Ecclesiastes 4:9-10*

8. "Lord, I give You thanks for renewing my mind and helping me see myself as a temple of Your Spirit." *Romans 12:2*

9. "God, I am grateful for the peace and joy You've filled me with

since breaking free from smoking." *Philippians 4:7*

10. "Thank You, Father, for turning my struggle into a testimony of Your power and faithfulness."
Revelation 12:11

www.ingramcontent.com/pod-product-compliance
Lightning Source LLC
Chambersburg PA
CBHW051356150726
48000CB00003B/1213